Let's Visit Spain

Susie Brooks

PowerKiDS press.

New York

Published in 2010 by The Rosen Publishing Group Inc.
29 East 21st Street, New York, NY 10010

First Edition

Library of Congress Cataloging-in-Publication Data

Brooks, Susie.
  Let's visit Spain / Susie Brooks.
    p. cm. -- (Around the world)
  Includes index.
  ISBN 978-1-4358-3027-1 (library binding)
  ISBN 978-1-4358-8608-7 (paperback)
  ISBN 978-1-4358-8609-4 (6-pack)
  1. Spain--Description and travel--Juvenile literature.
  2. Spain--Juvenile literature. I. Title.
  DP17.B75 2010
  914.604'83--dc22

                    2008051890

Manufactured in China

Note to parents and teachers
The projects and activities in this book
are designed to be completed by children.
However, we recommend adult supervision
at all times since the Publisher cannot be
held responsible for any injury caused
while completing the projects.

Web Sites
Due to the changing nature of Internet
links, PowerKids Press has developed
an online list of Web sites related to
the subject of this book. This site
is updated regularly. Please use this
link to access this list:
www.powerkidslinks.com/world/spain

Picture Credits
p5: © Tim Pannell/Corbis; p6: © Jose Fuste Raga/Corbis; p7: © John Eder/Getty; p8: © Hans Georg Roth/Corbis; p9:
© Arne Pastoor/Getty; p10: © Don Klumpp/Getty; p11: © Rob Cousins/Robert Harding World Imagery/Corbis; p12:
© Michael Busselle/Robert Harding World Imagery/Corbis; p13: © Manfred Mehlig/Getty; p14: © Dusko Despotovic/
Corbis; p15: © Jeremy Green/Alamy; p16: © Tom Grill/Corbis; p17: © Michael Busselle/Corbis; p18: © Alan Copson/
JAI/Corbis; p19: © Martin Barraud/Getty; p20: Martin Barraud/Getty; p21: © Ian Dagnall/Alamy; p22: © Nik
Wheeler/Corbis; p23: © Claire Shanahan; p24: © Jochem D Wijnands/Getty; p25: Demetrio Carrasco © Rough Guides;
p26, title page: © Bob Krist/Corbis; p27: © Claire Shanahan; © Jerry Cooke/Corbis; p28: © Reuters/Corbis; p29:
© Pete Saloutos/Corbis; © Harry Rhodes/Wishlist Images 2008; p30: © wen Franken/ Corbis.

Cover: the Sagrada Familia Church, Barcelona, © Tom Grill/Corbis; sightseeing boats on coast of Ibiza, Spain,
© Manfred Mehlig/Getty.

Contents

This is Spain!

Spain is a big country in the far west of Europe. Most people who come here on holiday arrive by airplane.

Spain is jam-packed with fun places to visit. Look for them in this book.

The **Canary Islands** and the **Balearic Islands** belong to Spain.

FRANCE

Atlantic Sea

PORTUGAL

Santiago de Compostela

Pyrenees mountains

Barcelona

Costa Brava

Madrid

S P A I N

Valencia

Balearic Islands

Córdoba

Seville

Canary Islands

Costa del Sol

Mediterranean Sea

ALGERIA

Arriving in Spain is exciting. Look and listen for things that are different from home. To start with, you will need to change the time on your watch.

It's fun to take a camera to Spain.

The Spanish people speak really fast!

Speak Spanish!

hello/hi
hola (**o**-la)

please
por favor (por-fa-**bvor**)

thank you
gracias (**gra**-thee-ass)

5

Summer sun

If you visit Spain in the summer, it is sure to be hot. Some parts of the country get hotter than others—check the weather forecast before you go!

Lots of vacationers head for Spain's sunny beaches. This is Tossa de Mar on the Costa Brava.

Things to take

- sunscreen
- sun hat
- swimsuit
- pail and shovel

If you're not near the shore, an aqua park is a great place to cool off!

Madrid, the capital of Spain, can be scorching in the summer months. In July and August, many people move away to cooler places near the coast or in the mountains.

Winter fun

Spain is a good place to visit in the winter—parts of the country stay quite warm. In the far south and on the Canary Islands, you'll find sunshine all year round.

You can ride a camel on black sand on Lanzarote in the Canary Islands.

Winter in the mountains is cold and snowy. You can go to the beach in the morning and get to the mountains by the afternoon— but don't forget a change of clothes!

Skiing is popular in the Pyrenees mountains in northern Spain.

Speak Spanish!

sun
sol (sol)

snow
nieve (nee-**ye**-bay)

beach
playa (**ply**-ya)

9

A place to stay

Spain is dotted with pretty towns and villages.

Lots of people who visit Spain stay in city hotels or **apartments** near the sea. Vacation houses called villas are popular, too, usually in quieter spots.

Speak Spanish!

house
casa (**ca**-sa)
bed
cama (**ca**-ma)
bathroom
baño (**ban**-yo)

10

You could stay in a house with a roof patio, a tent near the beach, or even a giant castle!

Some people in the Spanish countryside live in cave houses.

I got the faucets mixed up—they had different letters on them! In Spain, C is hot (caliente) and F is cold (frio).

On the move

Driving around Spain is a good way to see the country. People drive on the right-hand side of the road. They toot their horns when they pass you.

In the Spanish countryside, farmers often use donkeys to carry their loads.

We drove through the mountains. The roads were really wiggly and I felt a little sick!

These **tourist** boats are taking people to a beach on the Balearic island of Ibiza.

To get to the Spanish islands, it is quickest to fly. Some people take a ferry to the Balearic Islands, or sail a yacht around the coasts.

Speak Spanish!

car
coche (**co**-chay)

boat
barco (**bar**-co)

train
tren (tren)

Amazing Madrid

Madrid, Spain's capital city, is right in the middle of the country. It is busy, noisy, and full of things to see.

Imagine living in the Royal Palace—it has 2,800 rooms! This is the Grand Dining Hall.

People in Madrid like to spend time in the city parks and squares. There are often musicians, puppet shows, and other acts to entertain them.

There's a fun park and zoo at the Casa del Campo. You can get there by cable car.

Don't miss

El Prado—a huge art museum

Plaza Mayor—the lively main square, with cafés and musicians

Parque Mágico—a park with bumper boats and a mini-racetrack

Magical buildings

For spectacular buildings, visit Barcelona! A famous Spanish **architect** named Gaudi lived here. Look for his fairytale houses and the Sagrada Familia church.

You can tell why some people call the Sagrada Familia the sandcastle church!

Climbing up inside the Sagrada Familia made me feel really dizzy—there was a twisted staircase with 400 steps!

16

This mosque in Córdoba is now used as a Christian church.

There are beautiful holy buildings in many other cities, too, including Seville, León, and Santiago de Compostela. Most people in Spain are members of the **Roman Catholic** religion.

Every year, lots of people walk for weeks to visit the cathedral at Santiago de Compostela.

17

Feeling hungry

Tasting new foods is part of the vacation adventure! A fun thing to eat in Spain is tapas. You get to try lots of snack-size dishes, from spicy meats to sweet treats.

Don't miss churros con chocolate—you dip doughnut sticks into thick hot chocolate.

Paella is made up of rice, meat, and seafood, cooked together in a big pan.

Paella is Spain's national dish. The Spanish people eat a lot of fish and seafood. They like to cook with plenty of garlic and olive oil—you will smell it!

On the menu

chorizo (cho-**ree**-tho)
spicy sausage

tortilla (tor-**tee**-ya)
potato omelette

pan (pan)
bread

19

Family time

After lunch, there is a break called a **siesta**, when many stores close and it is traditional to have a nap.

Spanish families love spending time together.

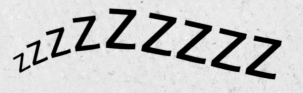

ZZZZZZZZ

Dinner is usually eaten after 9 p.m., so bedtime is late, even for the children!

In the evening, city streets come to life with families out together having fun.

We went shopping in the evening and I got to stay up till 11 p.m.!

Speak Spanish!

family
familia (fa-**mee**-lee-ya)
mom
madre (**ma**-dray)
dad
padre (**pa**-dray)

Let's go shopping

Markets are some of the best places for shopping in Spain. Look for colorful stalls of fruits and vegetables that are grown in the Spanish countryside.

On Sundays, the enormous Rastro market in Madrid sells everything from old clothes to wild animals!

The money you spend in Spain is called the euro. Try to buy something you can bring home as a **souvenir**.

Spain is famous for its hand-painted pottery. Pick your favorite piece!

Speak Spanish!

shop
tienda (tee-**yen**-da)

market
mercado (mare-**ca**-do)

money
dinero (din-**air**-ro)

23

In the wild

Spain is full of wide open spaces where farm animals and wild animals roam.

Visit the Doñana National Park and you might spot a rare Iberian lynx.

Look for

flamingos—Andalusia
monkeys—Gibraltar
ibex (mountain goats)—Pyrenees
dolphins—in the sea!

It's fun to go for a bike ride, pony trek, or camping trip in the hills of **Andalusia**. You'll see lots of olive trees. Farther south in Almeria, the land is very hot and dry, like a desert.

Don't miss Mini-Hollywood in Almeria— it's a real-life movie set!

Be a sport!

It doesn't take long to notice that Spanish people are crazy about soccer! Water sports, mountain biking, and basketball are also popular.

Learning to windsurf is exciting in the Spanish sun!

We went to watch a soccer game at the Barca stadium in Barcelona. It was so huge, it took us ages to find our seats!

Bullfighting has taken place in Spain for hundreds of years. This fight is in Seville.

Bullfighting is a traditional Spanish pastime that some people think is cruel. Most cities in Spain have a bullring with thousands of seats.

This poster is for a bullfight in Benalmadena in southern Spain.

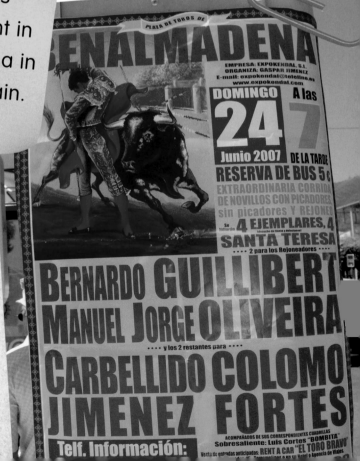

PLAZA DE TOROS DE
BENALMADENA
EMPRESA: EXPOKONDAL, S.L.
ORGANIZA: GASPAR JIMENEZ
E-mail: expokondal@telefono.es
www.expokondal.com
DOMINGO   A las
24 7
Junio 2007   DE LA TARDE
RESERVA DE BUS 5 €
EXTRAORDINARIA CORRIDA
DE NOVILLOS CON PICADORES
sin picadores Y REJONEO
Se torearán 4 EJEMPLARES, 4
SANTA TERESA
···· 2 para los Rejoneadores ····
BERNARDO GUILLIBERT
MANUEL JORGE OLIVEIRA
···· y los 2 restantes para ····
CARBELLIDO COLOMO
JIMENEZ FORTES
ACOMPAÑADOS DE SUS CORRESPONDIENTES CUADRILLAS
Sobresaliente: Luis Cortes "BOMBITA"
Telf. Información: Venta de entradas anticipadas: RENT A CAR "EL TORO BRAVO"

Party time

Many people try to visit Spain during a festival, or fiesta. Fiestas happen all over the country, and each region has its own special party.

In Tomatina in Buñol near Valencia, people throw tomatoes at each other for fun!

Fiestas often include **flamenco** dancers. They stamp their feet, twirl around, and play little wooden instruments called **castanets**.

Flamenco dancers wear fancy costumes. Listen for the click of their castanets!

Famous fiestas

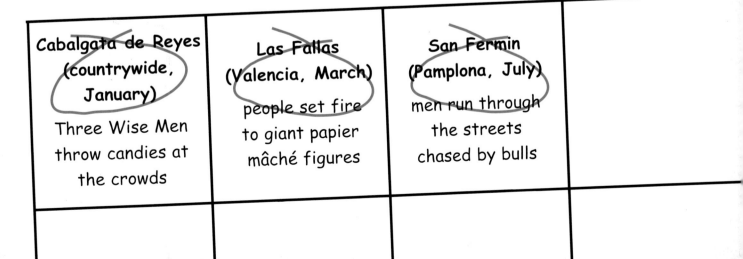

Cabalgata de Reyes (countrywide, January)	Las Fallas (Valencia, March)	San Fermin (Pamplona, July)	
Three Wise Men throw candies at the crowds	people set fire to giant papier mâché figures	men run through the streets chased by bulls	

Play it yourself

Try this Spanish playground game! It is a simple version of pelota pared, a sport invented in the Basque region of northern Spain.

In real pelota, people hit the ball with special bats strapped to their hands.

Pelota pared (wall ball)

You will need:
- a tennis ball
- chalk
- an outside wall
- 2 or more players.

1. Draw a chalk line across the wall, at about waist height.

2. Player 1 bounces the ball once, then hits it using a bare hand at the wall above the chalk line.

3. Player 2 lets the returning ball bounce once on the ground, then hits it back at the wall in the same way.

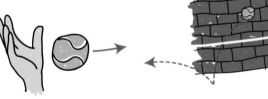

4. Players take turns as above.

You are OUT if the ball bounces more than once on the ground or the ball hits the wall below the chalk line.

TIP: You could play with five lives— one for each letter of the word "burro" (Spanish for donkey)!

Useful words and further information

Andalusia	An area in southern Spain.
apartment	A room or rooms to live in.
architect	Someone who designs buildings.
Balearic Islands	A group of Spanish islands, including Majorca and Ibiza, which lie to the east of Spain.
Canary Islands	A group of Spanish islands, including Lanzarote and Tenerife, which lie off the northwest coast of Africa.
castanets	Small musical instruments made from two hinged pieces of wood that the player clicks together in one hand.
flamenco	A traditonal type of Spanish music and dance that was invented in Andalusia.
Roman Catholic	A type of Christian. Catholics worship in churches and cathedrals.
siesta	The Spanish afternoon break, usually taken between 2 p.m. and 5 p.m.
souvenir	Something you take home to remind you of somewhere you have been.
tourist	Someone who is on vacation or sightseeing.

Books to read

Countries of the World: Spain by Kathleen W Deady (Capstone Press, 2000)

Living in Spain by Su Kent (Sea to Sea Publications, 2007)

Looking at Spain by Jillian Powell (Gareth Stevens Publishing, 2007)

Spain by Martin Hintz (Children's Press, 2004)